The Ultimate Book
of
Dog Cartoons

Featuring Cartoons From
Air Mail
Esquire
The New Yorker
and more!

Front Cover illustration: Jack Ziegler
Introduction: Bob Mankoff
Book Design: Darren Kornblut

Dedicated to Jennifer, Bea & Sadie

Cartoon Collections, LLC
10 Grand Central, 29th Floor
New York, NY 10017

For cartoon licensing information visit www.cartoonstock.com
Create a personalized version of this book at www.cartoonstockgifts.com

First edition published 2022

ISBN: 978-1-963079-04-3 / Item # 46498

Introduction

Bob Mankoff, former Cartoon Editor of *The New Yorker* magazine, here. For over twenty years as Cartoon Editor, I poured over thousands of submissions each week, critiquing, editing, and helping select those that would go in the magazine.

You might be surprised to know that that was not always a laugh fest. First, even the best cartoonists produce their fair share of clunkers, just like even the best baseball players often strike out–especially if they're on my team.

One kind of cartoon, however, could always lighten the mood. A good dog cartoon! When one of those came across my desk, I would get very excited and pat it and smooch it, saying, "Who's a good dog cartoon?", "Who's a good dog cartoon?" "You are! You are!" And what you've got here awaiting you as you turn these pages is even better. So much better. A whole book of very good dog cartoons from *The New Yorker*, *The Wall Street Journal*, *Barron's,* and *Air Mail.*

As a dog owner and lover, I really relate to these cartoons, and you will too. I guarantee it! 100%! And if that doesn't work for you, 75%! Really, these cartoons are as loveable and relatable as the smoochy pooches we adore, some with classic dog monikers like Fido, Rover, Cheeks, Spike, Barkley, and Duke, as well as more unusual ones like Pixel, Mochi, and Chair. Actually, I made that last one up, but I bet someone has named their dog Chair.

I hope you enjoy these cartoons while curled up with your little (or big) furbaby.

DOG FOOD GROUPS

GOOD

BAD

VERY BAD

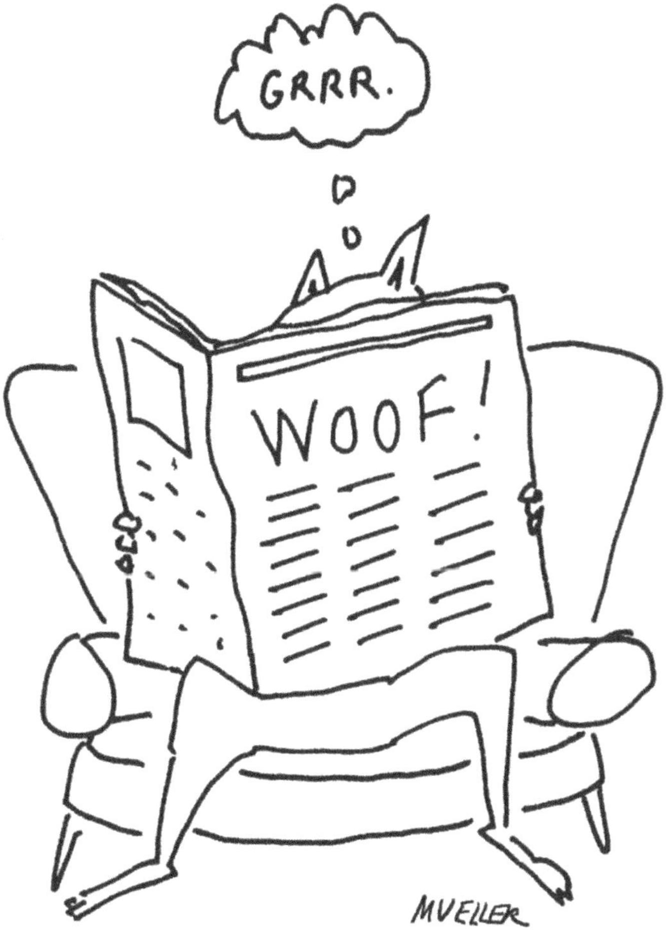
GRRR.
WOOF!
MUELLER

DOG DETECTIVES

"I just keep asking myself, 'what are we not sniffing?'"

"If you're never going to give me any, then quit calling it a doggie bag."

"There are no bad dogs. Only good dogs who make bad choices."

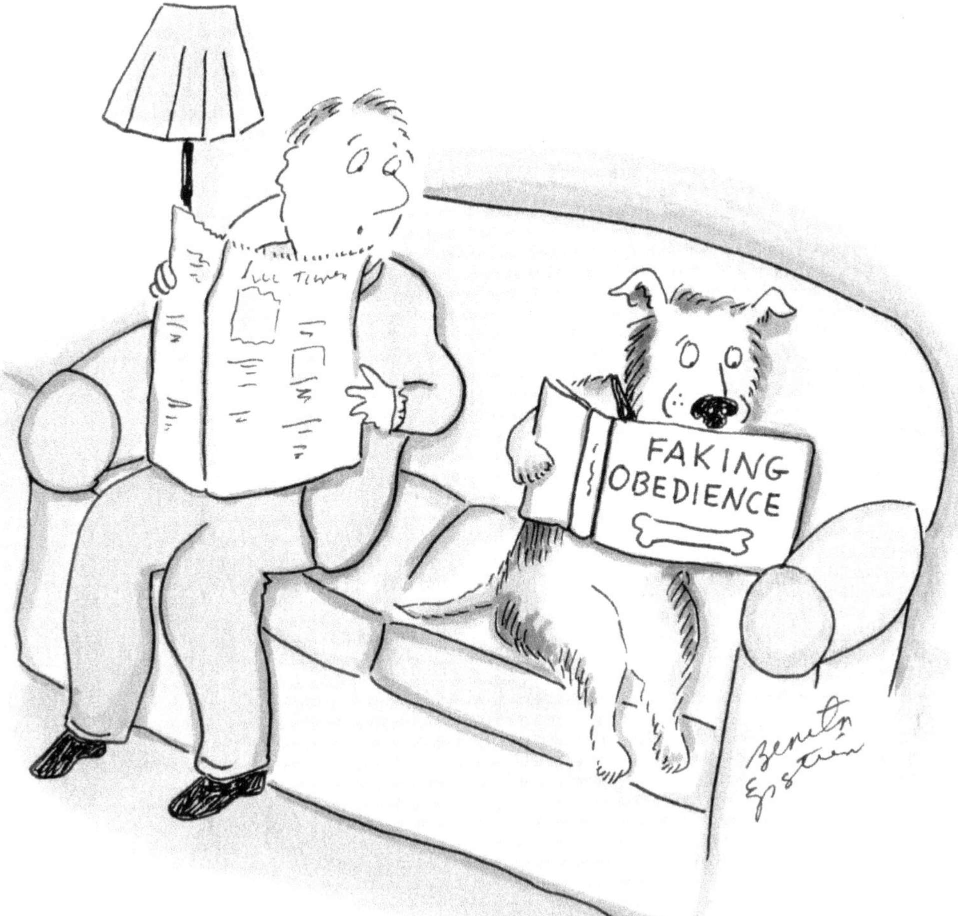
FAKING
OBEDIENCE

"I miss you too, honey. Now put the dog on."

"I had my own blog for a while, but I decided to go
back to just pointless, incessant barking."

FOOD   WATER   TIPS

GREGORY

"I can't wait until I'm old enough to dress myself."

"*Let's try it again. This time with a tad less mania.*"

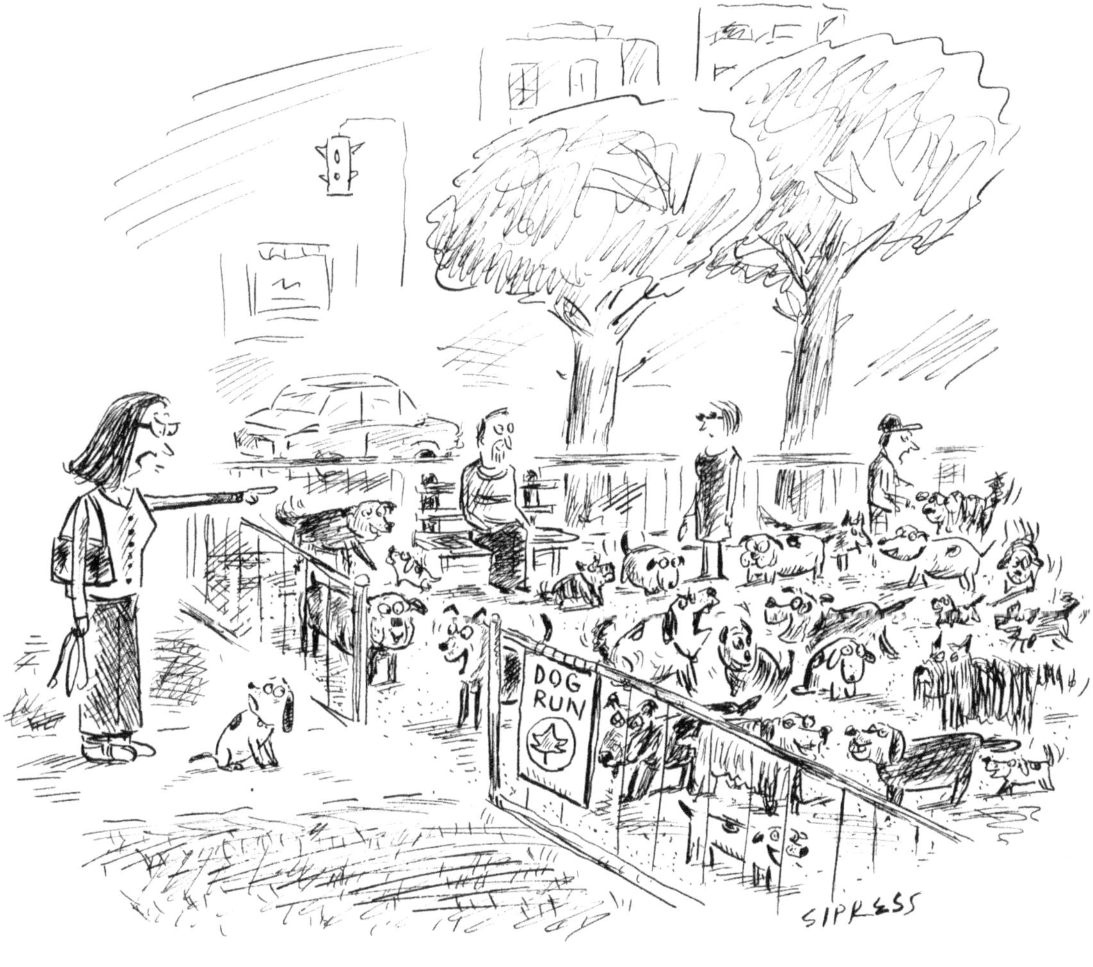
DOG RUN

"Schmooze!"

"You'll have to phrase it another way. They have no word for 'fetch.'"

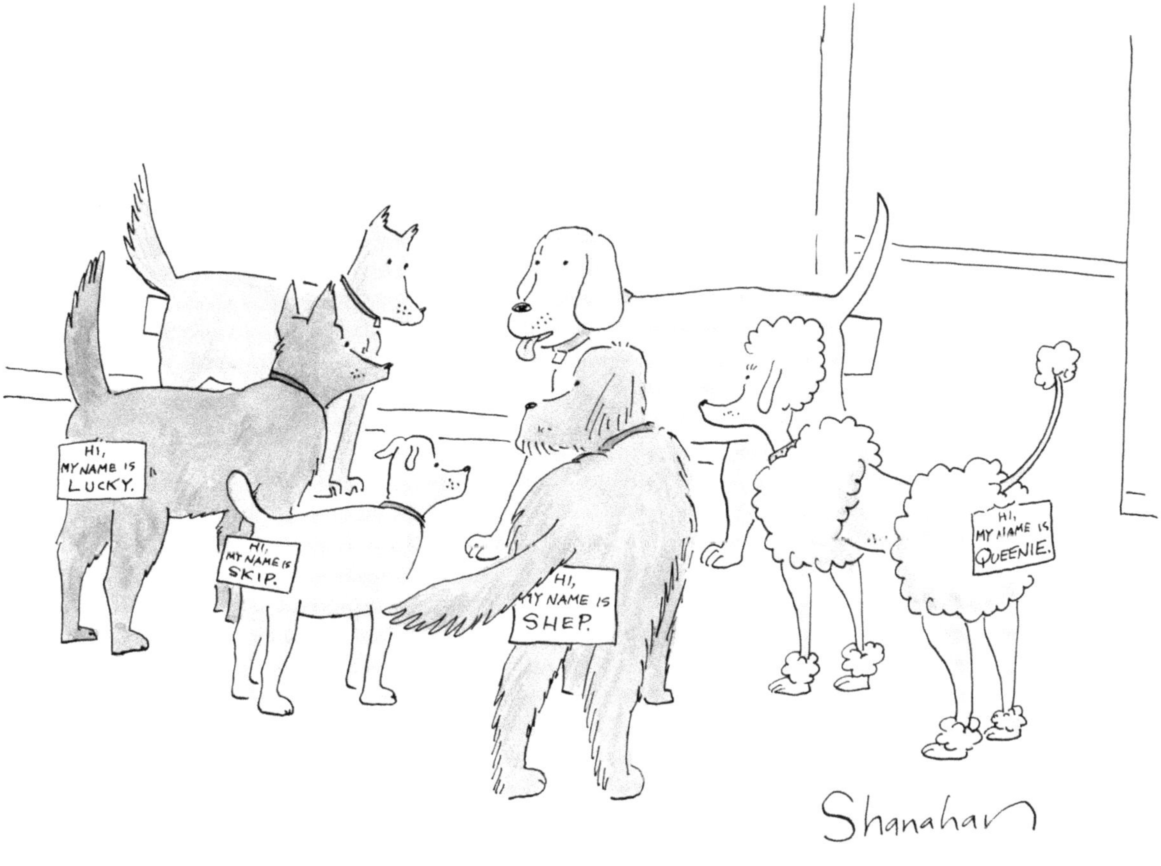
HI,
MY NAME IS
LUCKY.
HI,
MY NAME IS
SKIP.
HI,
MY NAME IS
SHEP.
HI,
MY NAME IS
QUEENIE.
Shanahan

"That's the problem with e-mail - no one to bite."

"They seem friendly enough so far."

DIFFEE

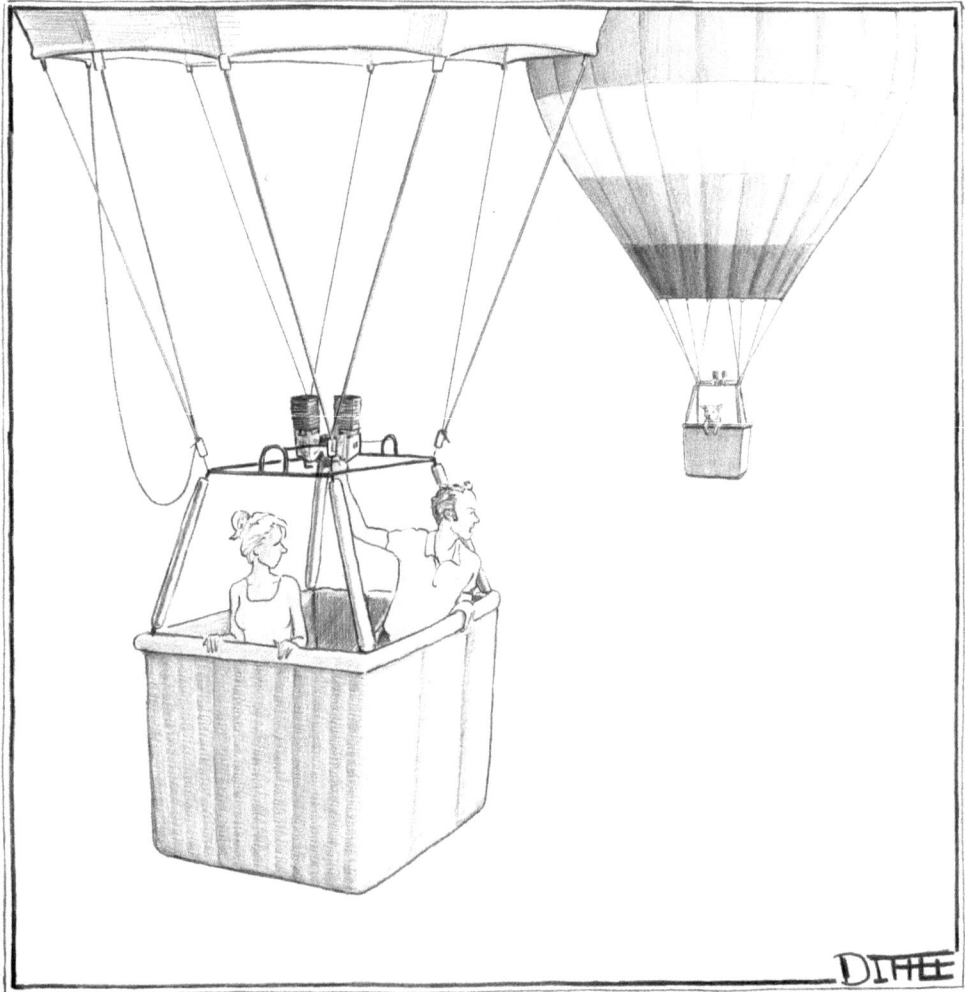

"No. Go home."

"*After you've wished once for food, you can stop using your other wishes on food.*"

"'It'll never work. You're a dog person and I'm a cat person."

"Kennel changes a dog, Muffin."

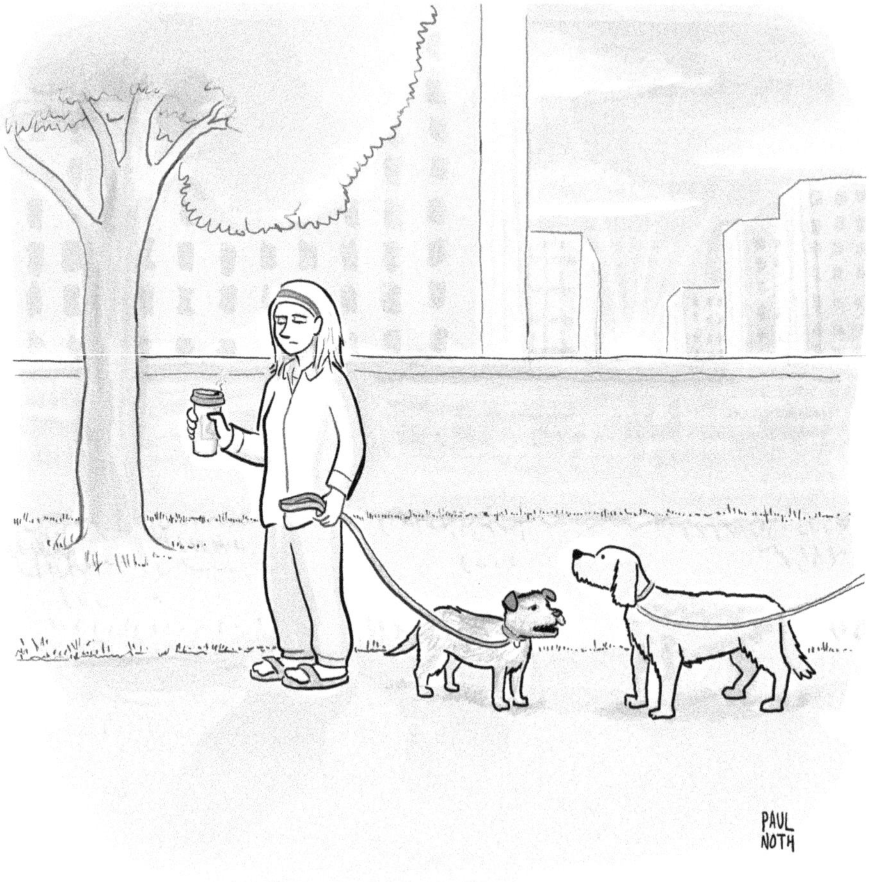
PAUL
NOTH

"She was a rescue."

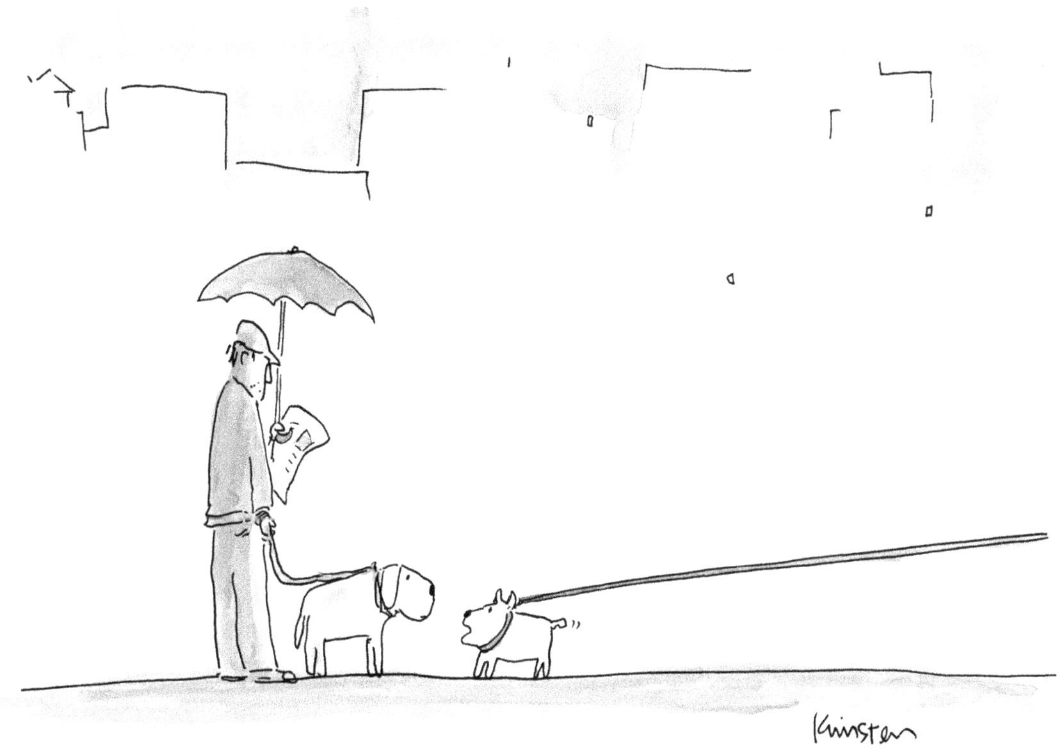
Kinsten

"Mine's still in bed."

"Are they still following us?"

"Yes, I came back. I always come back."

"'Is that all you can think about?"

"On the Internet, nobody knows you're a dog."

"Howard, I think the dog wants to go out."

"I bit someone once. It tasted like chicken."

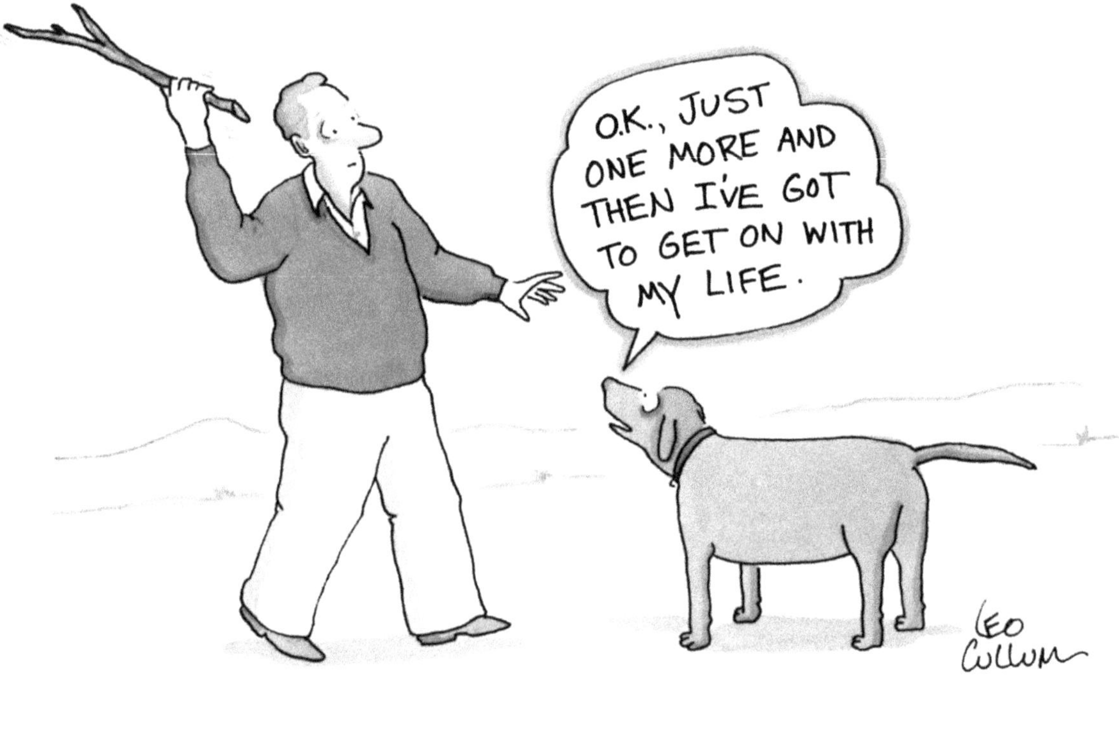
O.K., JUST ONE MORE AND THEN I'VE GOT TO GET ON WITH MY LIFE.
LEO CULLUM

"If you lie down with pugs, you wake up with pugs."

"You know your dog better than I do."

DOG WALKER TO THE STARS

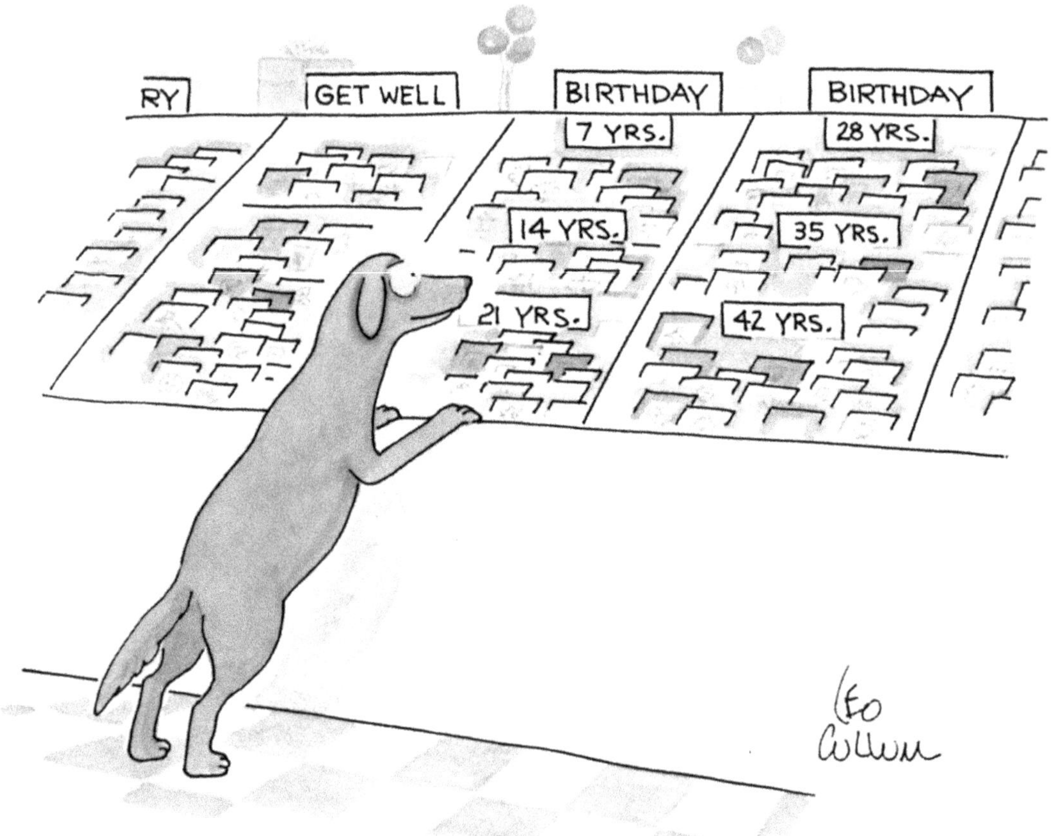
RY
GET WELL
BIRTHDAY
7 YRS.
14 YRS.
21 YRS.
BIRTHDAY
28 YRS.
35 YRS.
42 YRS.
LEO CULLUM

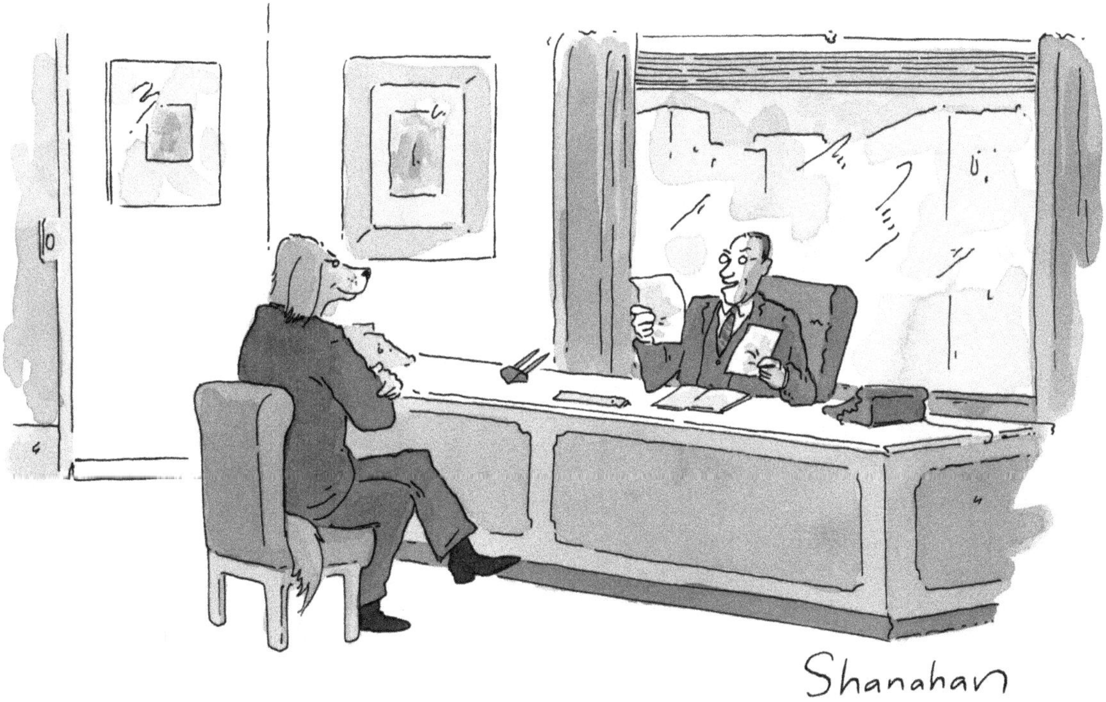
Shanahan

"You eat dog—excellent!"

"I started out fetching."

ZIEGLER

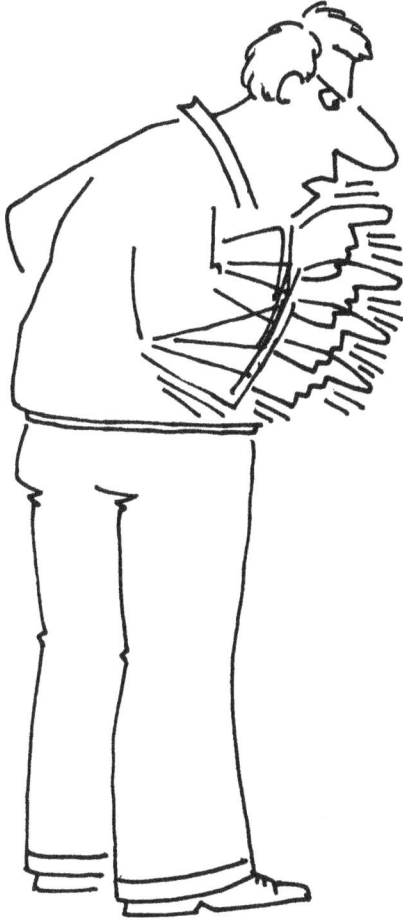

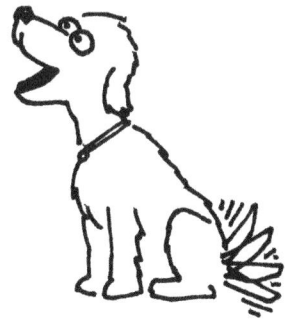

"It's always 'Sit', 'Stay', 'Heel',—never
'Think', 'Innovate', 'Be yourself'."

"Surprise!"

"*You will be going on a long walk.*"

"The leftovers sound good."

"You only think you're barking at nothing. We're all barking at something."

LASSIE! GET HELP!!
Shanahan

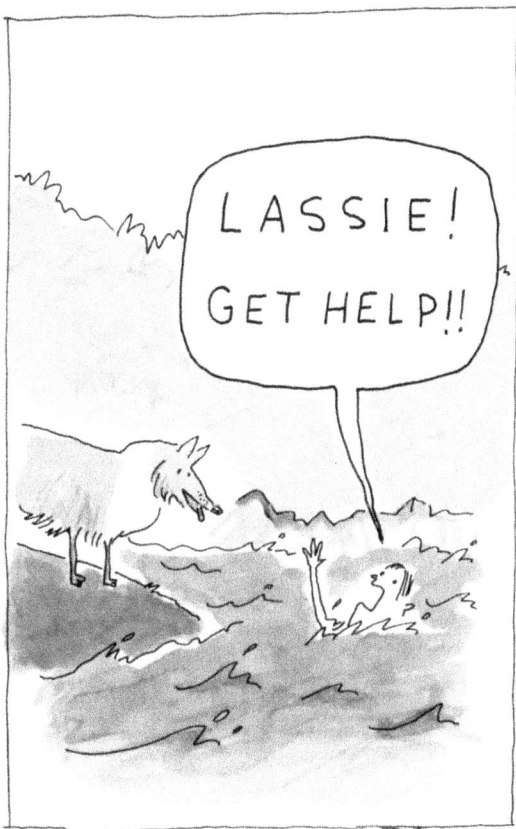

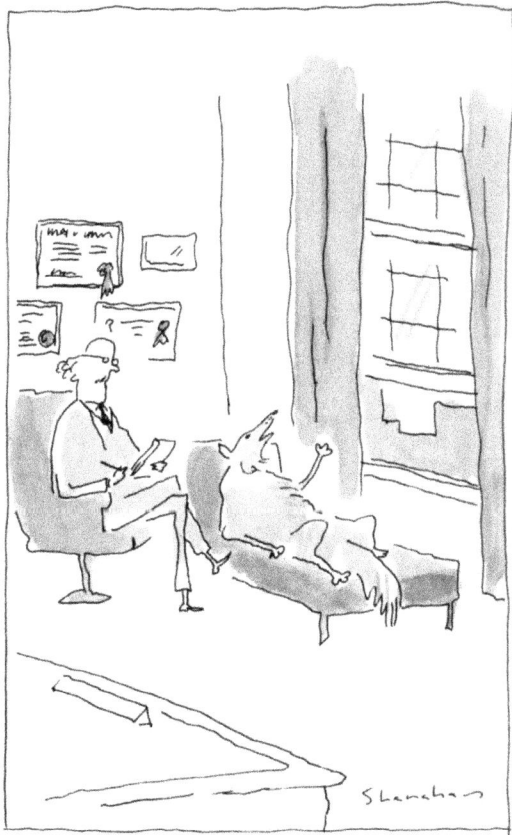

"Yes, I'm talking to you. I believe you're the only Sparky in the house."

"It's not enough that we succeed. Cats must also fail."

"Scotch and toilet water?"

"Not guilty, because puppies do these things."

"It's just the architect's model, but I'm very excited."

"My advice is to learn all the tricks you can while you're young."

"The bidding will start at eleven million dollars."

"O.K., I'm sitting. What is it?"

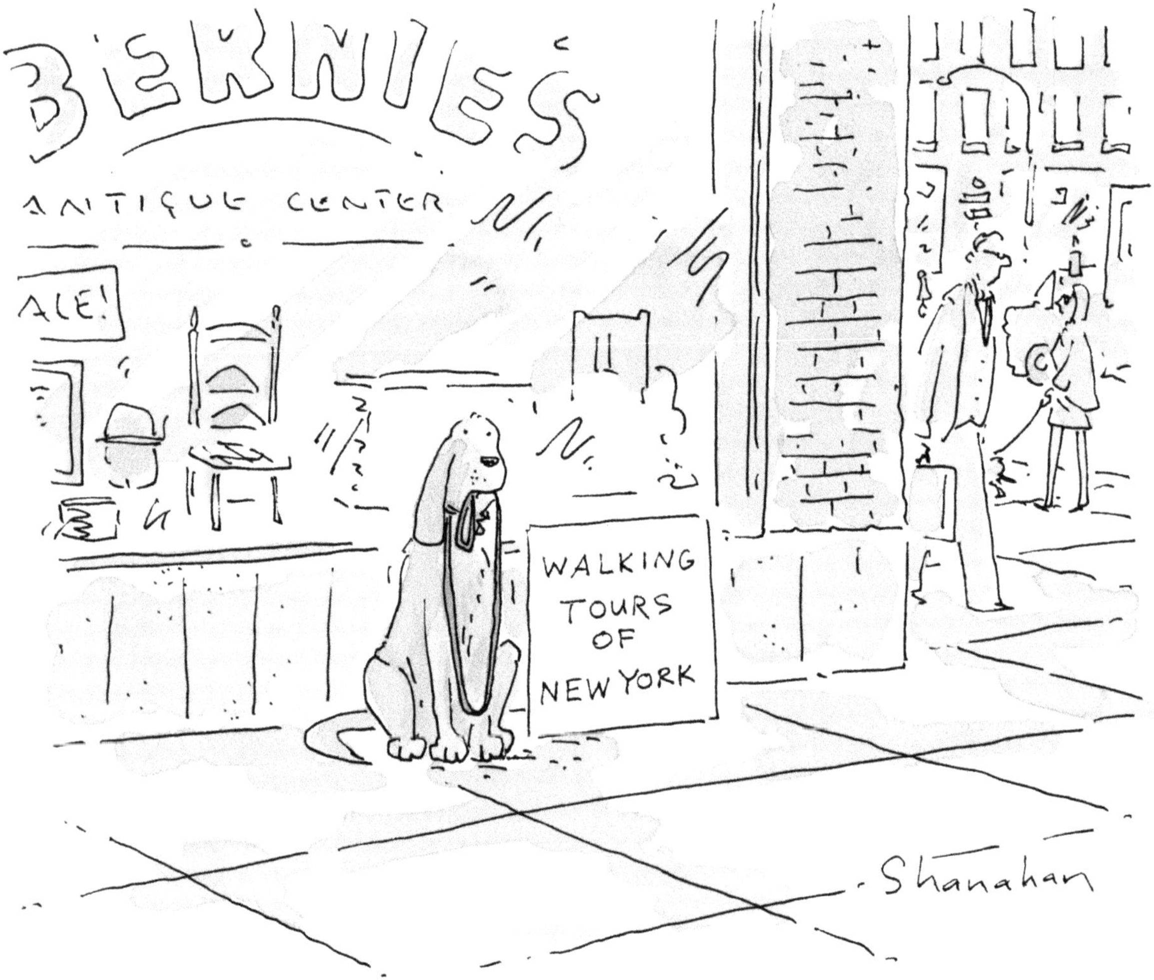
BERNIE'S
ANTIQUE CENTER
ALE!
WALKING TOURS OF NEW YORK
Shanahan

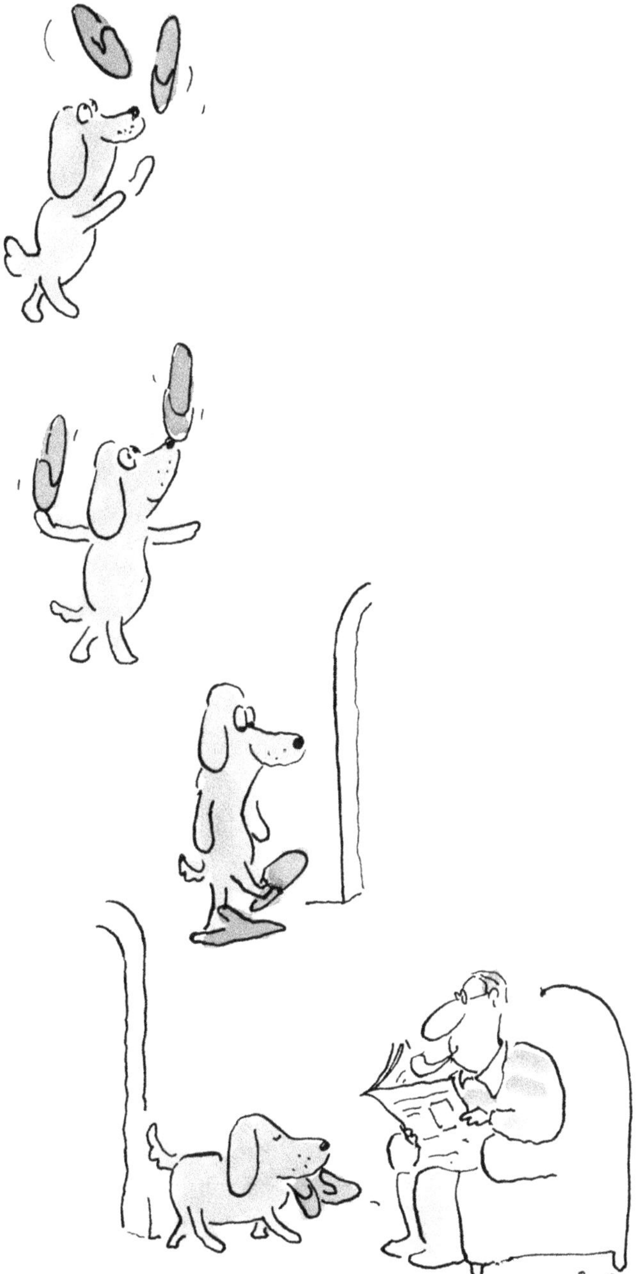
LEVIN

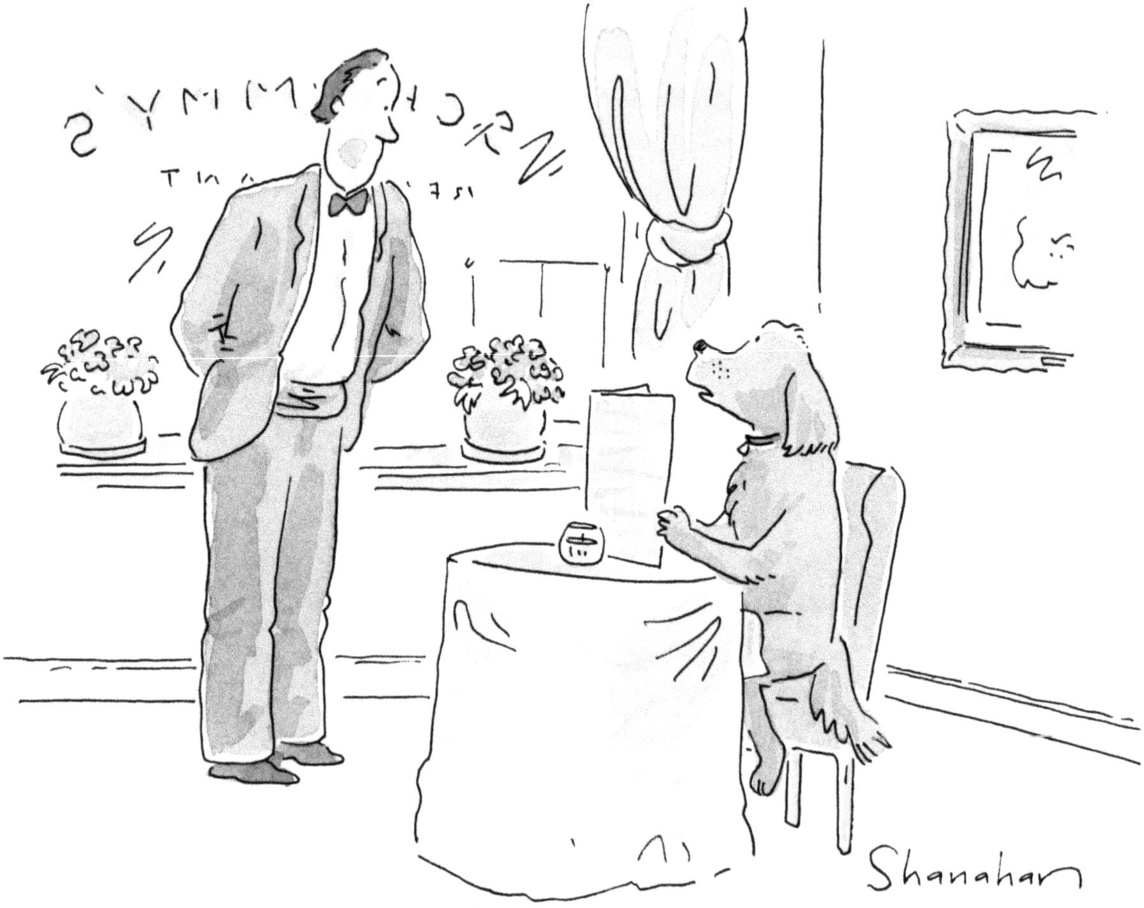
Shanahan

"Is the homework fresh?"

IT'S ALWAYS 'GOOD DOG'—
NEVER 'GREAT DOG.'
GREGORY

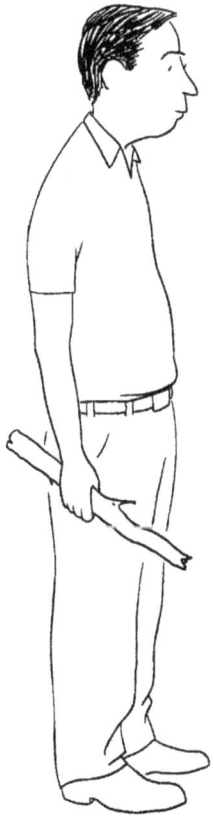

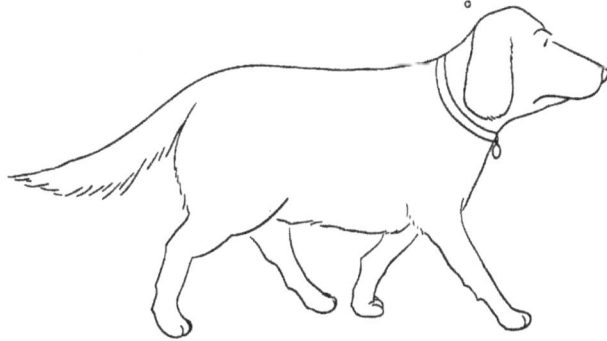

"On the plus side, you've cured my back pain."

"Yes, *they are crazy, but they can open the fridge.*"

"They were, sitting around the dinner table, knocking off a bottle of Cotes-du-Rhone and blathering about the Middle East—you've never heard such shallow, simplistic reasoning in your life—and one of them turns to me and says, 'And what do you think, Barney? What do you think we should do?' and all I could come up with was 'Woof'. I felt like such an ass."

"*Jimmy Choo, Mahnolo Blahnik—honestly can't taste the difference.*"

"I think we're named after computer passwords."

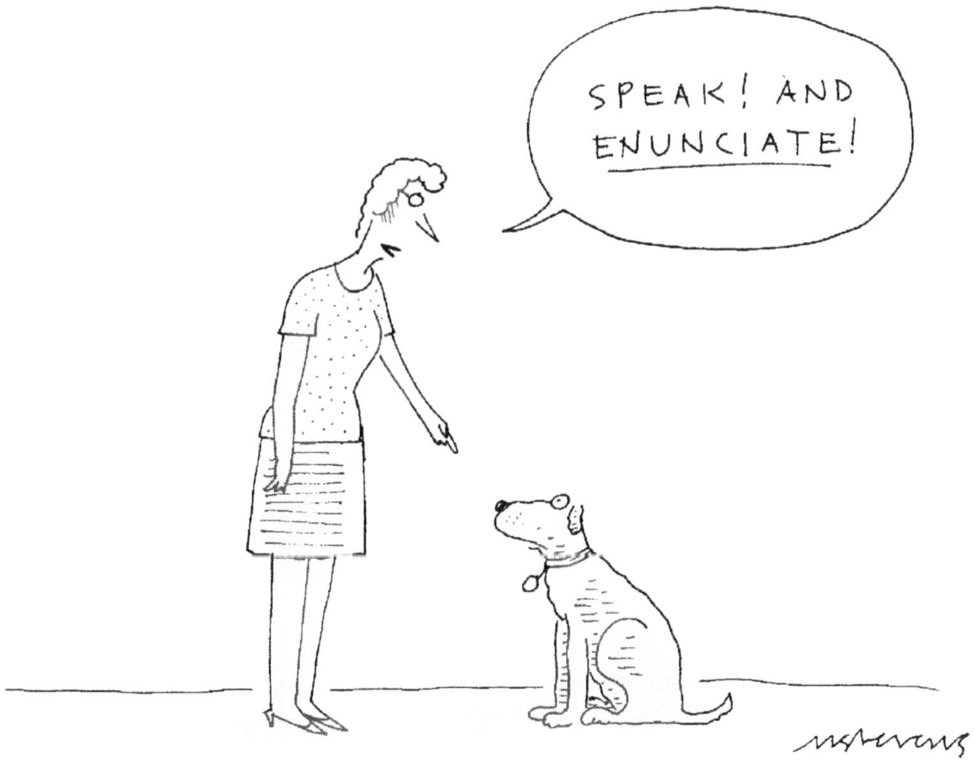
SPEAK! AND ENUNCIATE!

TEACHER'S PET

"One day, you'll look back on all your youthful mistakes and remember how adorable you were while making them."

"Look, Jake, I like you, but I can't be your best friend AND your agent."

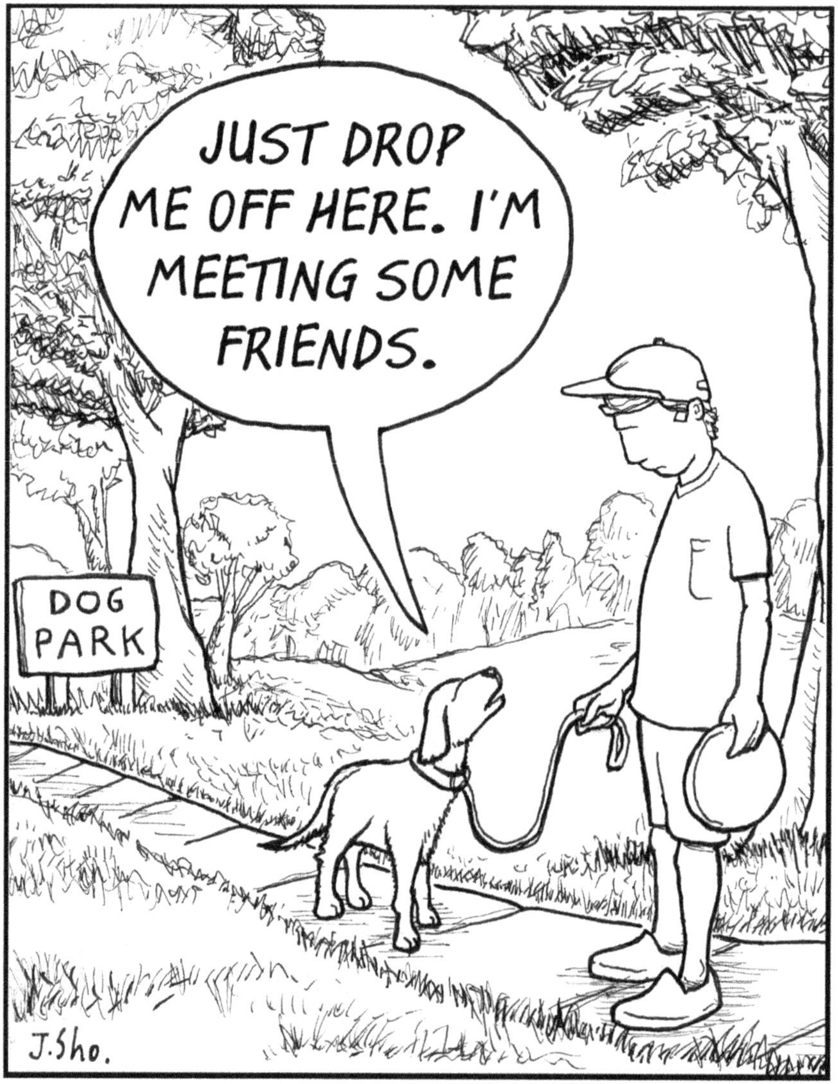
JUST DROP ME OFF HERE. I'M MEETING SOME FRIENDS.
DOG PARK
J.Sho.

Dog Teenagers

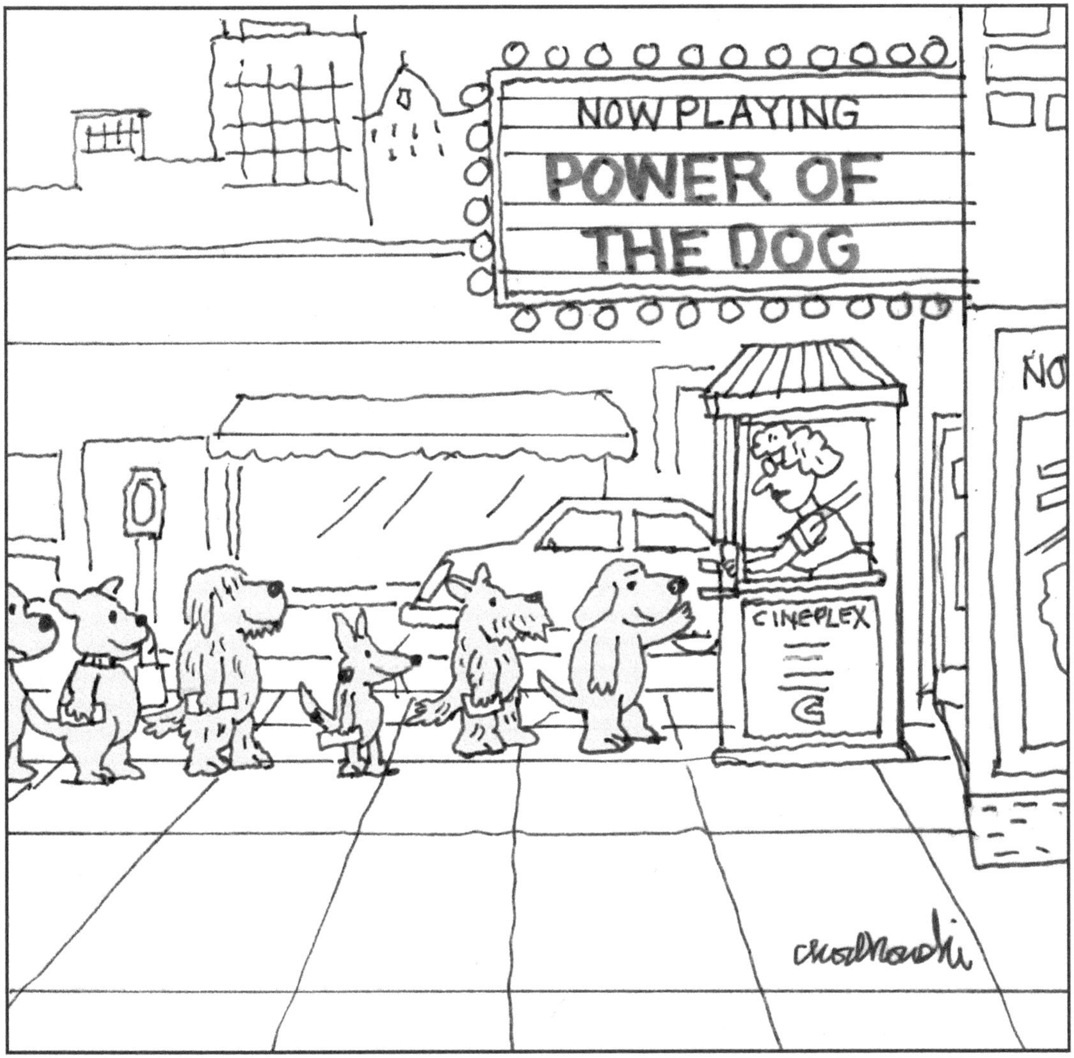
NOW PLAYING
POWER OF
THE DOG
CINEPLEX
NO

"Did you feed the dog?"

"Puppy love."

"I see high school, college, and business school, but I don't see obedience school."

"*Your Honor...he's a good boy!*"

"*Your Honor...he's a good boy!*"

"*Just pay attention and you might learn a few new tricks.*"

"No, I'm not faking it, I'm really happy when they come home."

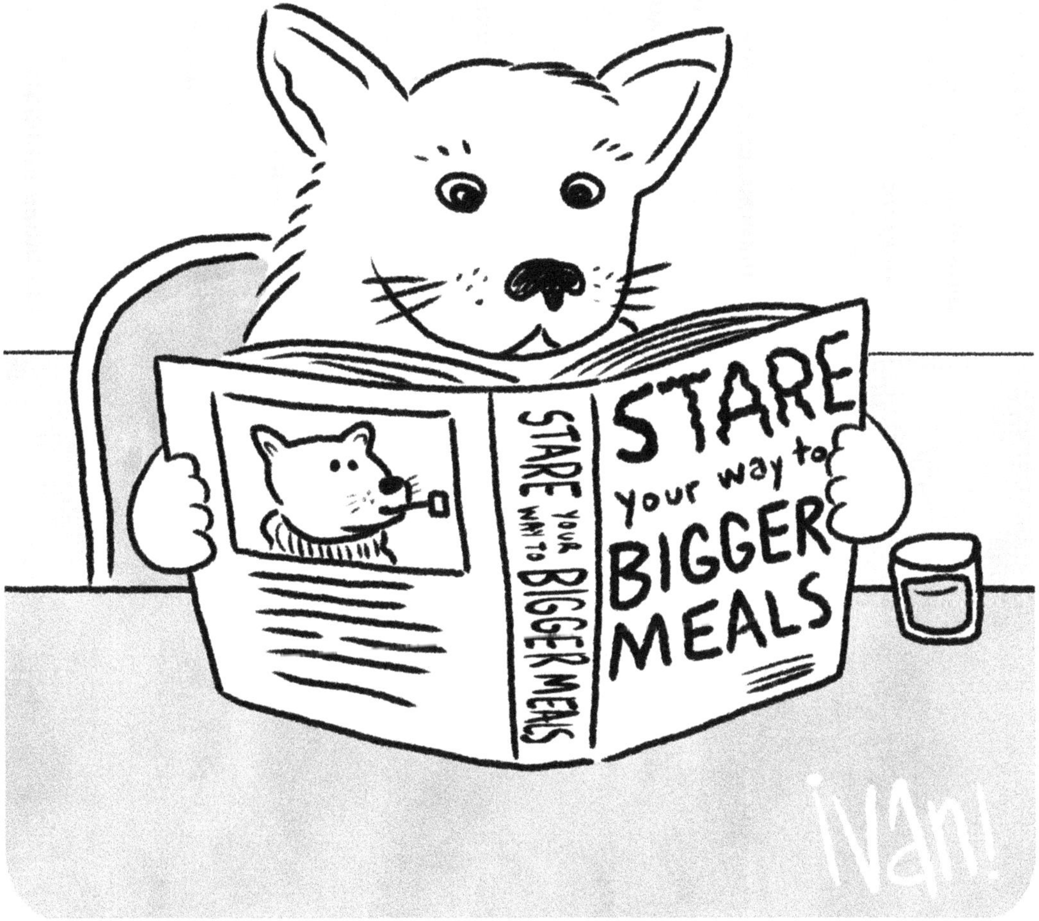
STARE your way to BIGGER MEALS
STARE your way to BIGGER MEALS
ivan!

THE EMOTIONAL
ROLLERCOASTER OF A LAB

INTROSPECTIVE

PANIC

MANIC

MURDEROUS

"I told you I'm not into any kinky stuff."

"The applications are limitless."

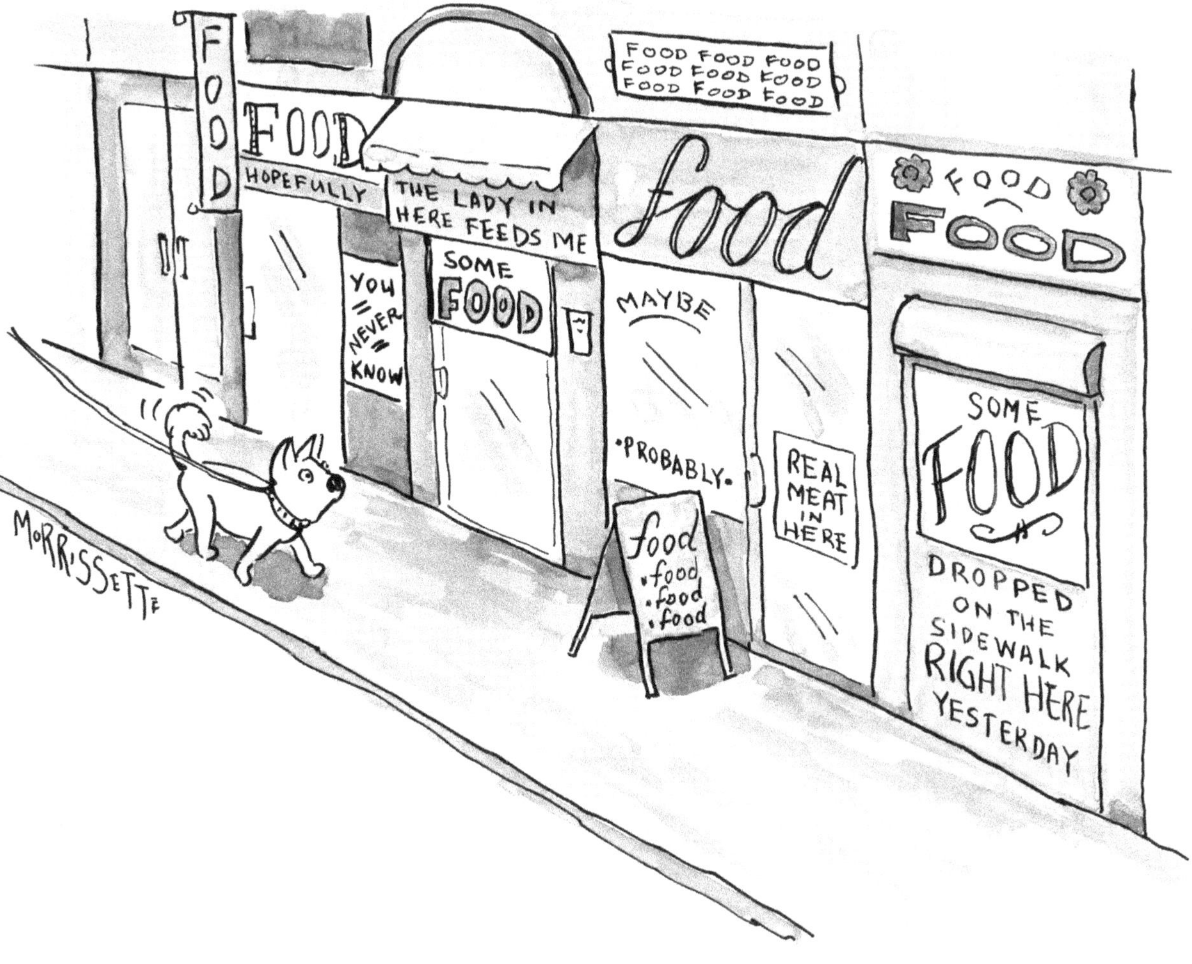
FOOD
FOOD
HOPEFULLY
THE LADY IN HERE FEEDS ME
YOU NEVER KNOW
SOME FOOD
FOOD FOOD FOOD
FOOD FOOD FOOD
FOOD FOOD FOOD
food
MAYBE
•PROBABLY•
food
•food
•food
•food
REAL MEAT IN HERE
FOOD
FOOD
SOME FOOD
DROPPED ON THE SIDEWALK RIGHT HERE YESTERDAY
MORRISSETTE

"My Instagram feed is basically people, dog food and tennis balls."

"Sorry honey, I'll be late. The boss told me to stay."

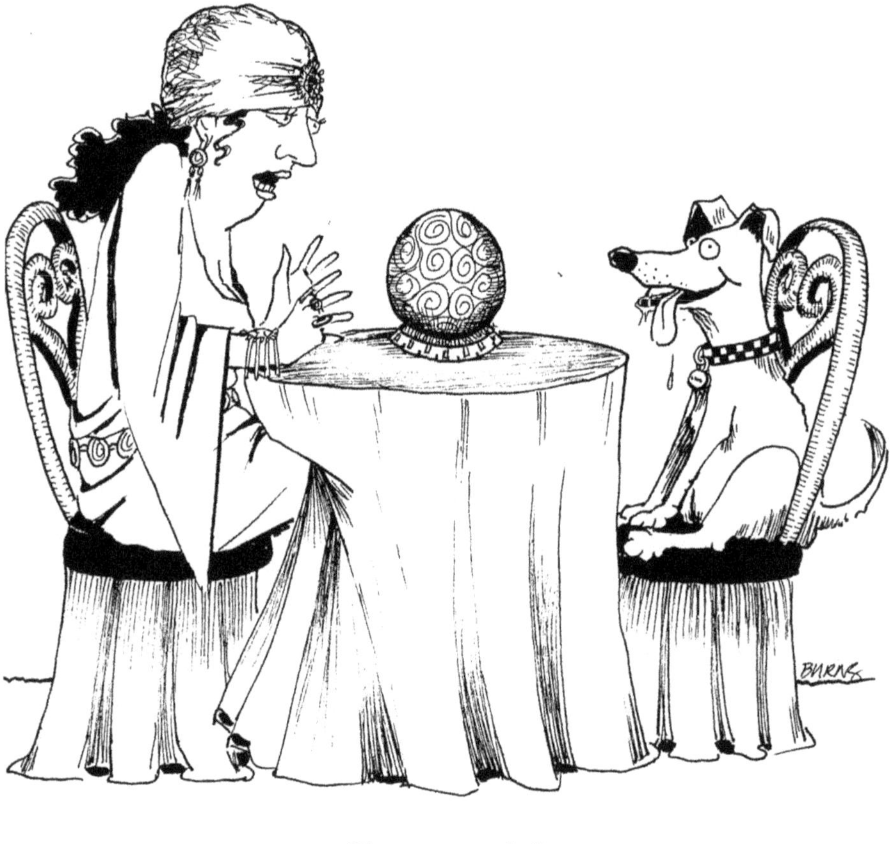
BURNS

"I see a couch."

"Now, I would like to introduce Buster, who woke up one morning and decided he wasn't going to let a 'Beware of Dog' sign define him."

"Package deliveries on Sundays? That makes the weekend so much more exciting."

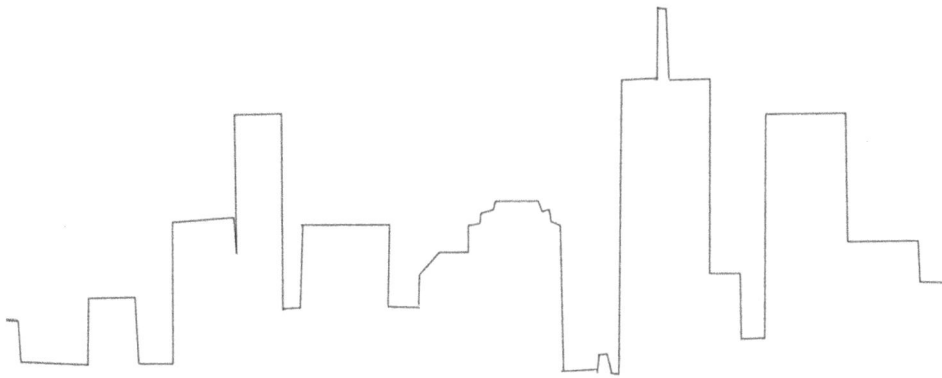

"It may be a dog-eat-dog world, but, personally, I'd prefer a good risotto with a glass of Riesling."

"Let's break the record for non-stop deranged barking."

"The only reason I come here is because they won't let me lay on the couch at home."

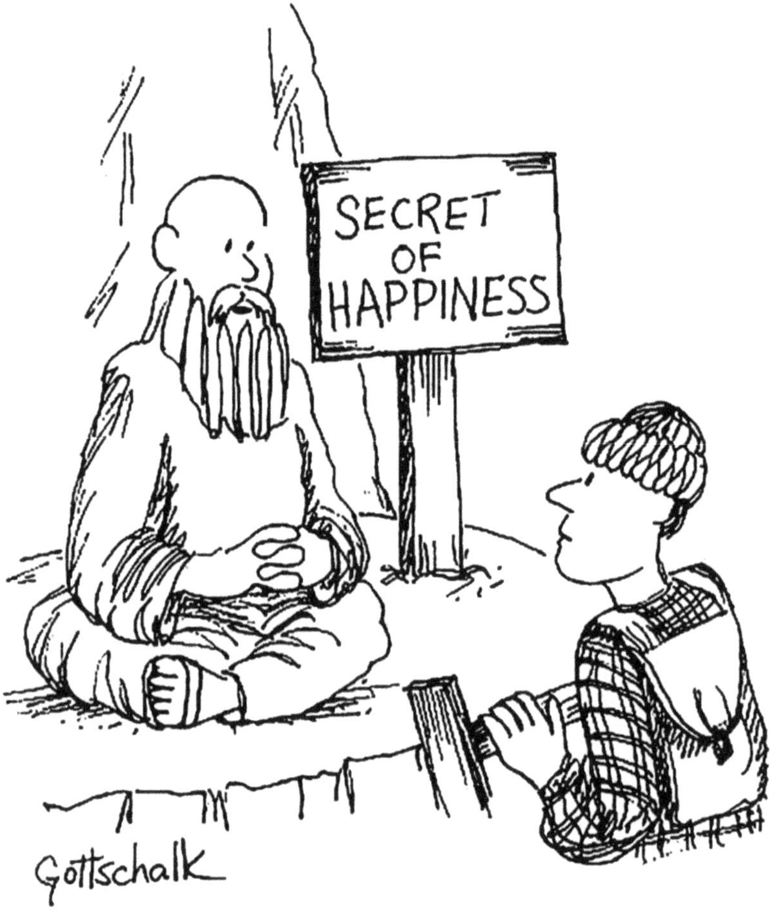
SECRET OF HAPPINESS
Gottschalk

"Get a dog."

"Meet my first dog. I've named him 'Security Question'."

"Bitsy and I decided controlling our portions wsa no way to live."

Index of Artists

www.ingramcontent.com/pod-product-compliance
Lightning Source LLC
Chambersburg PA
CBHW060759150426
42813CB00058B/2743

* 9 7 8 1 9 6 3 0 7 9 0 4 3 *